The God of Jesus
—Our God?

The God of Jesus
—Our God?

Alexander J. M. Wedderburn

CASCADE *Books* • Eugene, Oregon

THE GOD OF JESUS—OUR GOD?

Copyright © 2014 Alexander J. M. Wedderburn. All rights reserved. Except for brief quotations in critical publications or reviews, no part of this book may be reproduced in any manner without prior written permission from the publisher. Write: Permissions, Wipf and Stock Publishers, 199 W. 8th Ave., Suite 3, Eugene, OR 97401.

Cascade Books
An Imprint of Wipf and Stock Publishers
199 W. 8th Ave., Suite 3
Eugene, OR 97401

www.wipfandstock.com

ISBN 13: 978-1-62564-481-7

Cataloging-in-Publication data:

Wedderburn, A. J. M.

The God of Jesus—Our God? / Alexander J. M. Wedderburn.

viii + 80 p. ; 23 cm.

ISBN 13: 978-1-62564-481-7

1. Jesus Christ—teachings. 2. God—Biblical teaching. 3. Jesus Christ—Historicity. I. Title.

BS544 W43 2014

Manufactured in the U.S.A.

New Revised Standard Version Bible, copyright © 1989, Division of Christian Education of the National Council of the Churches of Christ in the United States of America. Used by permission. All rights reserved.

Contents

Preface   *vi*

1. The God of Jesus   1
2. The Nature of God
   —an Unanswerable Question?   17
3. The Nature of God
   in Christian Tradition   29
4. And Our God?   43

For Further Reading   79

Preface

Every so often scholars will produce works designed for a general readership and stripped of those aspects of their academic work that might confuse or distract this group of readers, namely such standard features of academic works as the footnotes, cross-references to other secondary literature, and evaluation of the work of other scholars. Perhaps this will be accompanied by the remark that any specialist who may read this particular work will be able to recognize that the author has not simply written the whole off the top of her or his head, but has had in mind the scholarly questions raised in the work in question and that there is an unspoken dialogue with other scholars being carried on between the written lines. There is a valuable contribution to making the results of scholarly work available in an uncluttered fashion to a far wider readership, yet, if I succeed in achieving this result, it will be first and foremost for a very different reason, one forced upon me: I have practically no access to any secondary literature except my own works and what I could glean, with caution, from the internet. This is the result of illness, but has the advantage from my point of view that any progress made may be rather quicker—a considerable advantage when one's work has already once been abruptly cut short, and this latest contribution is written

Preface

by virtue of a reprieve, so to speak. It may be cut short again, but I wanted to make use of the opportunity to try to tie up one or two of the loose ends left by my book *The Death of Jesus*, even if the attempt misfires and leaves me tied up in yet further knots (although tying knots is a common enough way to deal with loose ends). For I shall certainly be all too clearly out of my depth, but with a question such as the one raised here, the existence and nature of God, who could honestly claim not to be out of her or his depth?

I am very grateful indeed to the publishers Wipf & Stock and Cascade Books for accepting this work with all its shortcomings and would like to thank their staff, and above all, Dr. Robin Parry, for all their help and kindness in seeing this work through its final stages.

A. J. M. Wedderburn
Munich, 2014

ONE

The God of Jesus

Posing questions is no failing, especially in the context of a critical search for the truth, where critical questioning is an integral and essential part of this search. Yet some readers will perhaps think that the title of this work contains one question too many. For many hold that the God of Jesus *is* our God and our God *is* the God of Jesus. Nor need this "is" be only that which we use when we set side by side the photographs of a baby and of a person in their nineties and affirm that the one *is* the same person as the other, however much the outward differences may seem to outnumber the similarities. Many would claim that their God "looks (just) like" the God of Jesus, so to speak, and allow what Jesus reportedly said about God and the view of God implicit in what he said to determine their view of God.

Jesus in the Jewish World of His Time

Yet it must be remembered that Jesus was a man of his times and shared at least many of the views of his Jewish contemporaries, including many of those about God and the divine nature. If, however, those views were not fully uniform, then Jesus would have had at least to opt for the one or the other, and we see signs of this in the brief comments of Jesus attributed to him in Luke 13:1–5: over against the implicit view that those that suffered a violent end were particularly sinful in God's eyes, Jesus takes the cases of those who had been cut down at the orders of the Roman governor Pilate and those crushed by the collapse of a tower. They were no more sinful than others. The corresponding positive version of this view of God is found in Matthew 5:45 when Jesus assures his hearers that God grants the blessing of sunlight to wicked and good alike and that of rain to the righteous and the unrighteous. Implicitly Jesus shares here Judaism's view of a creator God who sustains and cares for this world, a conviction that comes to expression in a number of passages in Jesus' teaching (e.g., Matt 6:30/Luke 12:28). Yet the version of this belief that Jesus here propounds is one in which the creator God is a creator who does not discriminate between the righteous and the unrighteous in the distribution of the blessings of creation, and this presumably implies that the distribution of the woes of creation and of life in it alluded to in Luke 13 is equally even-handed, as that text in fact presupposes. This view of the impartiality of the creator God has to be set over against the view that it is the righteous whom God allows to prosper, while it is the evil and wicked who suffer.

Again, while Jesus shared with his Jewish contemporaries the conviction that God would in the future judge the world, as we shall see, there were various ways in which this belief was formulated. The judgment could take place in this world or seem to take place there, or could be seen as happening somewhere else. It could correspondingly lead to a divine kingdom in this world, which may well be the implication when Jesus sees God's kingly rule *already* bursting into this world in Jesus' earthly ministry, or it could lead to a new heaven and a new earth—if in fact the latter were in the last analysis to be distinguished from a *re*newed form of the heaven and the earth that we now have. For sometimes the *re*newal, if that is what is meant, is such that what is described could just as well be described as "new."

So we are told that some Sadducees—members of a Jewish religious group who, unlike many of their Jewish contemporaries, dispensed with belief in the resurrection of the dead—challenge Jesus with the question of a woman who, according to Jewish custom, after the death of her husband, was married, one after the other, to each of his six brothers: whose wife, they ask, would she be in the life that was allegedly to come? Jesus rebukes their lack of knowledge of the Scriptures and states that in the resurrected life one neither marries nor is given in marriage, but is like the angels in heaven (Matt 22:23–33). Whether this is "renewal" or "new," it is clear that, if it is meant to refer to a "renewed" earthly life, it breaks down conventional distinctions between heaven and earth. It is to be presumed that Jesus may have held some version of such an expectation, although it is by no means clear what, particularly if his followers may sometimes have superimposed their own view or views of the end on the tradition of Jesus' sayings. If Jesus indeed rejected the resurrection-less theology of the Sadducees, it is uncertain what view of the resurrection he held; at any rate, his followers, once convinced of his resurrection, gave different forms to this conviction, ranging from the mostly very this-worldly appearances in the first three gospels to the stress on the other-worldly in Paul's theology or the visionary experiences in Acts' accounts of Paul's conversion. It is, however, surprising when Luke has Jesus promise one of the criminals crucified with him that he would be with him *that day* in paradise (Luke 23:43), presumably, that is, in an other-worldly place that already existed distinct from this world; for the resurrection of the righteous or of all was usually expected to lie in the future, realized in an act of cosmic and universal dimensions, whether it took place on a renewed earth or in some transcendent realm. What would have been novel would have been the claim of Jesus' followers after his death that this final act, in whatever form was meant, had already taken place in the case of Jesus. Yet Jesus' announcement of the arrival of God's rule in this world at any rate suggests that his own inclinations lay in that direction, a renewal of *this* world, in contrast, say, to Paul who seems in 1 Corinthians 15:42–55 and 1 Thessalonians 4:15–17 to expect an other-worldly consummation. It is also to be assumed that Jesus' expectations had enough points of contact with those of sufficient numbers of first-century Palestinian Jews to make his message both intelligible and challenging for them, even if many today find such views either contradictory or incredible.

On the other hand, if Jesus and his message were to be intelligible to his audience, he must also have shared many of their other views and assumptions about God, and certainly many of the views concerning God and the ways of God attributed to Jesus seem to correspond to

The God of Jesus

those current in the Jewish thought-world of his day. It was, after all, the God of their fathers whose message he claimed to bring. Some of these views, however, are in many cases not ones that some Christians today would find attractive or acceptable. Jesus seems, for instance, to have shared the expectation of a final judgment in which God would condemn the wicked, presumably for ever, to a fate of torment, in which there would be weeping and gnashing of teeth (Matt 8:12; 13:42, etc.). It is true that this threat is more restrained, less lurid and vivid in its detail than the depictions of the fate of the wicked that we find in Jewish and early Christian texts that have not found their way into the canons of the Hebrew Bible and the Christian New Testament (not to mention the scenes of the last judgment painted in medieval art), yet its threat is nonetheless clearly recognizable. It is true that many Christians are still prepared to accept that their God is indeed like that and deals with humanity in this way. I recall how a conservative Old Testament scholar justified capital punishment on the grounds of his belief in a retributive God, and I am uncomfortably aware that parts of the New Testament would equally well support this belief. Nonetheless I could not and cannot believe in such a God, for the sake of consistency and integrity, although I am aware that many will say that I will all too soon discover my mistake and that the misgivings of my conscience were misplaced. It is true that, when Paul asserts that in Christ *all* will be made alive (1 Cor 15:22), he seems to give a different impression of a God who saves all, at least if the "all" made alive in Christ corresponds to the "all" who die in Adam, although the apostle's seeming universalism may be misleading here. For, while on the one hand he affirms that nothing can separate "us" from God's love in Christ (Rom 8:35), this "us" may be restricted to Christian believers; there is otherwise a seemingly unbearable tension between this passage and the predestinarian ideas found in Romans 9 and 11, where God elects some to life, but others to condemnation. Other passages in his letters seem to imply a future judgment on some, not just the fiery purging of the deficiencies of some Christian workers mentioned in 1 Corinthians 3:15, but something more permanent: for in Romans 2:5 and 8–9, there is reference to a day of God's wrath and just judgment, when affliction will come upon the wicked, and of those who have sinned it is simply said that they will perish (2:12; cf. also those destined to perish in 9:22).

At this point, however, we should already note in passing how important the criterion of coherence is for forming a judgment on the truth or the plausibility of an account, as we shall see later; for we seek to make assertions that are true or at least plausibly true and are not just wishful thinking. In the case of Jesus' preaching about God we find a God who acts in this world with impartiality towards righteous and wicked, but then in the coming world distinguishes sharply between them and assigns drastically different fates to them. It is hard to avoid the impression that God's whole character and the corresponding divine actions change radically as we move from this world to the next, and such an account seems to score rather poorly by criteria of coherence or consistency. The dissonance is such that one might be tempted to assign either the one or the other set of statements to Jesus' followers rather than Jesus himself. Yet both have their place within Jewish thinking of that

The God of Jesus

time, the one within the wisdom of the sages, or at least some of them (for other sages it was the righteous who prospered), as they reflected on the state of affairs of this world, the other within the reflections of apocalyptic seers as they assessed this world in the light of their convictions about the world to come. These two strands of thought existed alongside each other and at times intermingled. Either strand of thought *could*, therefore, have been read into the Jesus-traditions later, but equally both could have been taken over by Jesus himself. It is true that he would then have been seemingly oblivious to the dissonance involved here, but is that so unthinkable? To claim that it is runs the risk of making Jesus, if not omniscient, at least a rigorously logical thinker, and it is doubtful whether rigorous logic is an appropriate characterization of the style and content of Jesus' teaching.

If Jesus differed from his apostle on the question of how and when and where he expected this final consummation to take place, at least he could count on general agreement among most of his fellow Palestinian Jews. This was part and parcel of that sovereign rule of God that, if not so evident in his day in which the rule of the Romans and their client rulers weighed heavily upon the Jewish people, was expected to be revealed at the end. Indeed, much of the Jews' thinking about God, like that of other peoples at that time, was shaped by imagery drawn from the behavior of earthly rulers of the day. It is perhaps striking, then, that Jesus so seldom invokes this imagery in his parables, those narrative passages so characteristic of his teaching, which made certain points about God's character and about the nature of God's rule. That is true even of the image of God as king, despite the prominence in Jesus' teaching of references to the "kingly rule" or "kingdom" of God, a prominence that contrasts with the scarcity of equivalents to this particular phrase in Jewish literature of the time, despite its frequent references to God as king and as ruling. Nonetheless, the figure of a king or someone like one does sometimes appear. In Matthew 18:23 it is a king who calls his debtors to account. In Luke 7:41–42 it is a man who had two debtors and could seemingly afford to let them both off; yet his behavior, as in many of these stories, would strike Jesus' hearers as unusual. And in Matthew 22:2 it is again a king who invites guests to a wedding feast (but in Luke 14:16 it is simply a "man" who issues the invitation to a great feast; Matthew may be closer to the original polemical setting of the story, but adds a number of features to the story that, amongst other things, reflect the sack of Jerusalem around forty years later). In the light of the kings and rulers Jesus was faced with in his world—such as the ruler of Galilee, Herod Antipas, to whom Jesus refers, hardly flatteringly, as a "fox" (Luke 13:32), or the memory of Antipas' ruthless father, now dead, Herod the Great—it is perhaps no accident that such a figure played no *prominent* part in his depictions of God.

Less specifically, it may be a matter in some parables of a relatively powerful person who is described in such a way that some higher rank or social standing is indicated: it is only in Matthew's version of the story of the wicked tenants that the owner of the vineyard, who the tenants seek to appropriate, is described as the "master of a household" (Matt 21:33), although such a rank is also implicitly held by the "man" in the story according to Mark and Luke. At any rate, it is to be noted that the

The God of Jesus

behavior of this vineyard owner in rewarding the hired laborers with the same sum regardless of the time that they had worked is decidedly unusual and was calculated to startle those who heard the story. The father of the two sons in Luke 15:11–32 is also presumably relatively well off, with his hired servants and his property to divide between the sons, and again his conduct is surprising, being contrary to the expectations of both his sons: the one does not expect such generosity as is shown in his being restored to the privileges of sonship, the other feels himself slighted and regards such generosity as quite inappropriate. Finally, there occurs the figure of a judge, but in Luke 18:1–8 an unjust one, whose sense of justice is subordinate to his own convenience, a comparison that must have disconcerted Jesus' hearers.

Yet, however little Jesus drew on the analogy of earthly rulers to make his points about God and God's rule, and although he explicitly rejects those rulers' ways as a model for the behavior of his followers and their relationships to one another (Mark 10:42–44/Matt 20:25–27/Luke 22:25–26), nonetheless he seems to share with his contemporaries a view of God that ultimately draws on the model of the earthly plenipotentiary. So he tells his disciples in Gethsemane that for God anything is possible (Mark 14:36), even if he may have added, as he was arrested there a short time later, that God could have sent more than twelve legions of angels to rescue him, but implicitly chose not to do so (Matt 26:53). In fact, he was manifestly not rescued in that way, so that one may wonder whether later Christians, knowing that no such divine action had taken place, attributed these words to Jesus. In that case it is legitimate to ask whether Jesus himself was in fact so sure that God's hand would not be manifested to save him in this way. Had he such insight into God's will and plans that he knew that this was a possibility that would *not* be realized? Yet if others, such as the author of John's Gospel, portray Jesus as omniscient, this is not the case in Mark or Matthew, where neither the angels nor the Son know the time of the coming end, but only the Father (Mark 13:32/Matt 24:36). One has to explain, at any rate, why Jesus felt himself so left in the lurch and let down by his God as he hung suffering on the Roman cross (Mark 15:34/Matt 27:46). It could, of course, be that this cry of Jesus has been attributed to him later by two gospel writers, in stark contrast to the Johannine Jesus who, as the good shepherd, has the power to lay down his life and take it up again (John 10:18) and whose death is greeted with a triumphant cry of accomplishment (John 19:30); or, again, it contrasts with the ideal martyr displayed in Luke's account who expects to go to paradise and trustingly commits his life into God's hands (Luke 23:43, 46). Yet the version given in Mark and Matthew is so disquieting and disconcerting that it is hard not to believe that it is nearer the historical reality of Jesus' death, and that the other two gospels have therefore sought an alternative portrayal, one more congenial to their conceptions of the dignity of one who was God's Son.

At any rate, whatever Jesus expected to bring about by his suffering and death, it is clear that his teaching in general is to be set in the context of Jewish thought and expectations current in his day. It is, then, appropriate to ask, before we place too much weight on Jesus' view of God or make it too normative, whether we are prepared to take over uncritically the rest of the Jewish thought that

The God of Jesus

is the background to his thinking about God. For his view of God, however central to his message, was not unrelated to other beliefs, such as the election of Israel and its role in the divine purposes, that were part and parcel of Jewish tradition. Perhaps we need not demand that one version of such beliefs in its entirety must be presupposed, but sufficient must be presupposed in order to provide a framework within which Jesus' beliefs and teaching about God are intelligible. That is a particularly pressing question once we find that Jesus himself was prepared to adopt a critical stance towards much of this Jewish thinking and indeed had to if that thinking was not uniform and was disunited within itself. It becomes more acute if we find that what he did take over and accept may have led him astray, and may have led him to misunderstand God's will for him in those fateful last days in Jerusalem and to die in agonized disillusionment.

Jesus and the Fatherhood of God

Most Jews of that day thought of their God, too, in personal terms and addressed their God correspondingly, unless they were very much under the influence of Greek philosophy and preferred to speak of God as "the one who exists" or the like; such philosophically inclined Jews were, however, very much the exception. Jesus also spoke of God in personal terms, perhaps even more so than many of his fellows. For, while it is clear that talk of God's fatherhood was not unparalleled in Jewish writings of the time, Jesus' way of speaking of God as his "father" seems to have been not only more prominent but also more vivid and direct. Only once is the Aramaic "abba," meaning "father," put on his lips in the gospels, as Jesus prays in Gethsemane (Mark 14:36), but the usage was evidently memorable enough for Paul to use this Aramaic term twice, even when writing to Greek-speaking Christians (Rom 8:15; Gal 4:6), and it is presumably this term that lies behind the succinct "father" at the beginning of Luke's shorter version of the Lord's Prayer (Luke 11:2, in contrast to Matthew 6:9's wordier and more formal "Our Father in the heavens"). Contrary to the view of those who want to distinguish between Jesus' relationship to God and that of his followers, the usage of this prayer suggests no such distinction, but invites Jesus' followers to share his way of addressing his God; such a distinction may be intended by John 20:17, "I am ascending to my Father and your Father, to my God and your God," but the language of this gospel in general reflects the high status given to Jesus in the theology of this author and should not be taken as a guide to Jesus' own usage and self-understanding.

This usage of Jesus should not, however, be overvalued as unique. God is, for instance, addressed as "our Father" in the fifth, sixth, and nineteenth (!) petitions of the Eighteen Benedictions, an ancient prayer in daily use in Judaism, which echoes in places the contents of the far briefer Christian Lord's Prayer. Even the short "Father," without a possessive pronoun or other elaborations, is found in the Wisdom of Solomon 14:3, a Greek work found in the Old Testament Apocrypha and possibly stemming from Alexandria in the century before the beginnings of Christianity. Nor is the Aramaic word limited to the usage of a child speaking to its father as some have suggested. That might at first sight be a plausible suggestion in the light of Jesus' saying about the need to enter

God's kingdom like a child (Mark 10:15/Luke 18:17). Yet this mode of address was also used, respectfully, in speaking to older and revered men. So it is told (in a later rabbinic text, the Babylonian Talmud, tractate *Taanit* 23b) of a charismatic rabbi named Honi, who lived in the century before Jesus and was noted for the effectiveness of his prayers in moving God to send rain, that in a time of drought rabbis would send schoolchildren to him to take hold of the hem of his gown and say, "Abba, abba, give us rain!" That caused Honi to pray to God saying "Ruler of the world, do it for sake of these, who cannot distinguish an abba who can send rain, and an abba who cannot." Here one clearly sees how children use "abba" to address this revered man; whether only children used this term is not so clear. At any rate, Honi picks up their usage to refer to God, doing so in the third person and not as a direct address to God; his own way of addressing God is very different and far more exalted and reverential: "Ruler of the world."

Nonetheless, the frequency with which the fatherhood of God is referred to in the Jesus-traditions, even if we leave aside the Gospel of John, where it is particularly prominent and dominant, is striking and far in excess of the occurrence of this motif in contemporary Palestinian texts. Moreover, the simple "father" as the opening word of an address to God—even if it occurs far less frequently in the Jesus-traditions in the first three gospels than references to God as "father" in the third person—is even harder to parallel (in the Wisdom of Solomon 14:3, a Greek text, it is not the opening word).

At any rate, talk of God as "father" and prayers addressed to God as "father" imply a relationship between

The God of Jesus—Our God?

God and humanity that can be described as "personal." Yet could we have expected anything else in Jesus' world and time? In the Jewish tradition more abstract or impersonal ways of speaking of God were, as already mentioned, rare, except in circles influenced by non-Jewish philosophical traditions, and even in the Greco–Roman world the opposite was often to be found, namely the tendency to speak of abstract concepts such as "fate" or "fortune" in personal terms, treating them as personal deities. That should not surprise us, for we are accustomed enough to apply language appropriate to human beings metaphorically to inanimate objects (the sea raged, the election campaign is waking up) or even to address them as if they were human (like the sailor invoking the wind or the farmer the rain or the golfer talking to a little white ball), but without, of course, any inclination to treat them as divine (even the little white ball). It is true that there was also in the Greco-Roman world, at least among some of the intellectual elite, a tendency to scorn the antics and character of the anthropomorphic and all too human deities of their myths; if one did not simply dismiss those myths as worthless and corrupting, but wanted instead to salvage from them some intellectual and moral worth, then there were the possibilities offered by an allegorical interpretation of those myths, for instance seeing various deities as symbols of natural forces or the physical elements. Most of the contemporaries of these philosophers did not bother themselves with such sophistications and seem to have been fairly at ease with the human or rather more than human figures that peopled their mythological world. And in the world of first-century Palestinian Judaism, while the proliferation of deities and their ways amongst contemporary non-Jews might excite the scorn and indignation of Jews, anything other than the assumption that their God was personal and could be addressed as such would have been unthinkable and unintelligible. What may have been unthinkable then is, however, today a very live option, which may well be forced upon us by the problems that inevitably anthropomorphic ways of thinking and speaking of a personal God involve, so that we need to ask whether it is necessary to follow Jesus and his Jewish contemporaries in thinking and speaking of and to God in this way. For to assume that Jesus has said the last word on this matter involves recognizing and endorsing the role played by his religious and cultural background in shaping his beliefs and according at least some measure of a normative role to that background as well. I say "some measure of a normative role" in view of the diversity of that background and the way in which Jesus selected from the options that it presented him with, now adopting some, now modifying others.

Yet, if we are to cast aside views of God as an old man in some place called "heaven," where are we to turn in order to offer a view of a God that is "personal"? Distancing ourselves from God's fatherhood and other analogies to the divine nature drawn from oriental potentates is all very well, but the idea of a personal God then seems to slip through our fingers. For all our talk of "persons" and the "personal" is very much dominated by our experience of the admittedly elusive term "person" as applied to human beings. Some, shunning any such anthropomorphism will speak rather of God as a "force" or "power," but that too has its problems. We can speak of persons as "forces" (e.g., "X was a force for good in his or her community"), but it is doubtful whether we can meaningfully turn that around in order to talk of forces as persons, except perhaps in a very metaphorical sense. "Power" is beset with similar difficulties, but in this case may in addition raise the question whether we might not want instead to speak of God as "powerless" in the light of Jesus' death on the cross, bitterly complaining that his God had forsaken him.

Again, the adjective "personal" is a slippery one that can cause confusion here. For we often use it of things that belong to a (particular) person, such as personal possessions, personal memories (alongside such senses as "directed at a particular person," as when we speak of "personal" remarks or insults), but that usage will probably not help us here. It is true that one could speak of one's personal god or gods as in the case of the household gods or spirits of the ancient Romans, the *Lares*, which were peculiar to individual households or families. That is scarcely the sense intended here, for even in the case of Jesus it would be inappropriate to speak of him as regarding his heavenly Father as belonging to him or peculiarly his, especially if one does justice to the invitation, implicit in the Lord's Prayer, to all his followers to address this God as "father." Thus, within the general problem of an appropriate conceptualization of what we mean by "God," there is the more specific one of whether we can use the term "personal" here and in what sense. That is a question that we must constantly bear in mind in confronting the daunting and elusive question of the nature of God. It may be difficult enough to say anything of that nature, much more so to say that we can go further and appropriately describe it as "personal."

TWO

*The Nature of God—
An Unanswerable Question?*

Questions about the "nature" of persons or things are by no means all alike. For sometimes it is a question concerning the character of that person or thing. The nature of a thing may be, for instance, hard or soft, stable or unstable, visible or invisible, and so on. The "nature" of human persons may likewise be kind or cruel, honest or deceitful, diligent or lazy, or may manifest one or more of a countless number of traits. On the other hand, the question about the nature of a person or thing may be posed in a more philosophical way, so that answering it is rather a matter of definition or classification, placing that person or thing in a broader category. It may then be more a matter of "characteristics" rather than "character," as one can see from many dictionary definitions: thus a "table" can be defined as a flat surface resting on a number of legs or on some form of support, the flat surface and the supports belonging to the characteristics one expects of a table. If the flat surface is, say, suspended from the ceiling one may wonder whether it deserves the designation "table." With human beings this question is more difficult and yet must be posed if we are to distinguish them in any way from other animals. Most would want to do so, some much more drastically and clearly than others, although it is very clear that our race shares a great many physical and behavioral characteristics with many animals, the most with apes and monkeys and "higher" forms of animal life. Even if one avoids such problematic concepts as that of the "soul," it nevertheless seems that human beings possess certain characteristics—such as their capacity for self-reflection, self-criticism, and self-transcendence—that, at least as far as we know, separate them from other animals. Or, if other animals share these characteristics, then their presence is hidden from us. In that case, we would do well in our anxiety not to invoke what some have scornfully dubbed "the ghost in the machine" (i.e., the soul), to recall that there are levels and dimensions of the human person that are not simply confined to the material basis that enables those dimensions to function.

The Question of the Nature of God in the Ancient World and Its Legacy

Yet, even if this definition of human nature in this sense of "nature" works reasonably satisfactorily with human beings, the task becomes far more difficult when we ask about the nature of God, although that has not prevented the philosophically inclined from trying to do so down the centuries. And, although these unending philosophical and theological deliberations should have been warn-

The Nature of God—An Unanswerable Question?

ing enough, those arguing for or against the existence of God, often with a bitter and unyielding dogmatism on both sides, have to this day often given the impression that they know in advance what they are arguing for or against. Yet, as soon as we think of defining the nature of any entity in terms of classification or categories, the difficulty of the task becomes apparent: are we really to place God in a class or category along with other entities? Symptomatic of the difficulty is our uncertainty as to what pronoun is to be used when we speak of God, "he," "she," or "it," an uncertainty that raises far wider and yet more fundamental issues than feminist theologians' legitimate protests of the dominance of masculine pronouns in our talking about God. (Some other languages may be able to shelter behind grammatical rules that assign genders to each substantive, but English has no such hiding place.) Hence my striving to avoid personal and possessive pronouns referring to God in this work.

At any rate, philosophical quests for God, particularly those under the influence of the dominant philosophical traditions of the Greco-Roman world—above all, those of Plato and Aristotle—tend to start out from assumptions about God's nature very different to those reflected in the traditions of Jesus' teaching and work, and the conclusions to which they come differ correspondingly. For their view of God is essentially a static one, an unchanging God and one not susceptible to emotion or suffering. Such presuppositions made and make it difficult to do justice to either God's becoming flesh, at least as the doctrine of the incarnation was traditionally understood, or to what happened in Jesus' passion. The demands of such assumptions and philosophical traditions led to such strange strategies as the separation of a divine nature from a human one in Jesus, as we shall see presently in the definition of Christ's nature reached at the Council of Chalcedon in 451. These two natures, divine and human, were separated to such an extent that the former was considered eternal and unchanging (as God was and is) and only the latter came into being at the conception of Jesus and endured the suffering of his death. Needless to say, little of such sleight of theological hand is apparent in the Jesus-traditions, at least in the first three gospels. (John's Gospel, on the other hand, is overlaid with a great deal of theological reflection, though even here such a distinction and separation between Jesus' divine nature and his human nature is hardly explicit.)

The philosophical question became the more difficult and acute both for philosophers (and for Christian theologians who were greatly influenced by them) after Plato, in the fourth century before our era, unexpectedly and enigmatically described "the Good," which one otherwise might have thought to represent the apex of a hierarchy of being in the thought of that philosopher, as "beyond being" (*Republic* 6.509B). If the question of the nature of the divine is treated as a question concerning the "being" of God then Plato had obviously put the cat among the philosophical and theological pigeons. This gave the impetus to a tradition of mystical thought, both non-Christian and Christian, characterized in medieval thought by both apophatic and cataphatic ways of speaking and thinking about God: the apophatic denied that one could say anything about what God *is*, although one could say what God was *not*, the cataphatic showered upon God an abundance of metaphors drawn from all

The Nature of God—An Unanswerable Question?

sorts of contexts, many of them seemingly contradicting one another. Being metaphors, by their very nature these statements about God ascribed to God what God was not or what was not God, so that in the last analysis both the apophatic and the cataphatic came to a similar conclusion.

This Platonic tradition continues to present problems in more recent thought. This is the case, for instance, when God is conceived as the "ground of being" (or "being itself"), a term associated with the theology of Paul Tillich, a leading theologian of the twentieth century. It is, for a start, not clear that these two phrases mean or can mean the same thing. For can "being," even with the qualifying "itself," be meaningfully described as the "ground of being" without introducing the impression of a sort of circularity? Would one not expect that which is the "ground of being" to be something other than "being (itself)," something "beyond being" in Plato's words? Has one then, by means of this way of speaking, come further than that "learned ignorance" of which the fifteenth-century mystic Nicholas of Cusa spoke?

It is small wonder, then, that some philosophers and theologians speak of "the other" or "mystery" or the like where we might expect references to God. It is all the more evident in this usage that there is a problem about the content of these expressions and their claims to truth. On the other hand, the absence of a readily defined and assumed content is a great advantage when one remembers how often the nature of God is discussed in terms of a particular tradition of philosophy or theology and it is then at least implicitly assumed that one knows in advance what the characteristics of God are. Nonetheless, one has to ask how far the assertions that we make about God, the "other," or this "mystery" can claim to be true.

The Question of Truth and Its Criteria

Often the discussion about establishing claims to truth is posed in terms of the alternatives of the criteria of coherence or correspondence, but in many instances one might expect that both would have to be satisfied, in some measure or other. Historical statements and historical accounts, for instance, may be regarded as true or at least probably true if they meet both requirements. That Jesus was put to death by the Romans corresponds to the manner of his death, a Roman execution by crucifixion rather than, say, a Jewish execution by stoning to death; and there seems little reason to doubt that this was in fact the means by which he was put to death. (If, however, Jesus never existed, as some ultra-skeptics have sometimes claimed, then naturally this statement no longer has any claim to truth.) Moreover, the statement and the historical account in which it is contained, if it is to be a coherent one, will also need to show why the Romans meted out this punishment to Jesus, either in terms of the nature of Jesus' ministry and message or the interests of the Jewish and Roman authorities in silencing him, or preferably both at once. For, if there was nothing in Jesus' behavior to warrant such a reaction on the part of the authorities, and no discernible sense or motive on their part that led them to do this, then this could awake doubts as to the truth of this account. In fact, it seems clear that Jesus' arrival in Jerusalem had aroused popular expec-

The Nature of God—An Unanswerable Question?

tations and his action in the Jerusalem temple seems at first sight a very open challenge to the authority of the Jerusalem priestly aristocracy and thus to the stability of Roman rule in the province, which depended on the support and cooperation of that aristocracy. (With the accounts of Jesus' resurrection appearances, on the other hand, the situation is very different: the accounts themselves differ considerably in their contents, and various features like the failure to recognize the risen Jesus or the whole question of the identity of the risen Jesus with the earthly raise doubts as to the coherence of these accounts. Nor is it quite clear to what they would correspond, for the various references to the resurrection appearances, as already mentioned in the previous chapter, sometimes seem to presuppose a very tangible, corporeal encounter, sometimes a more visionary experience.)

The question of God's nature seems at first sight, however, to be something quite different that cannot be resolved by such means. It is true that the criterion of coherence does come into play, inasmuch as we are called upon to give a coherent account of this God in relation to the world and our experiences of it and in it. Yet we have already seen difficulties seemingly arising here, with a God that acts impartially in this world but then metes out very different treatment to just and unjust in a coming world. By and large, at any rate, it seems to be chiefly with criteria of coherence that systematic theology has traditionally operated, without too much attention to the counterbalancing questions of correspondence. That has doubtless led to some impressive accounts of Trinitarian theology and soteriology, but leaves many with the uneasy impression of something constructed on a foundation that today seems more than a little suspect. On the empirical level, too, coherence may well present problems. For instance, in the shape of experiences of natural disasters, pain, and evil, which do not seem to fit in with some traditional beliefs about God's nature—in particular, God's love and omnipotence. Yet, even if we succeed in giving a coherent account, correspondence may prove a more difficult criterion to satisfy. God is invisible, perhaps even incomprehensible if many mystics are right, and there are no manifestations of divine existence and power that are beyond all questioning and doubt. Historical statements' claims to truth and the basis upon which they rest at first sight do not seem to be applicable or helpful here.

God—A Historical Question?

The Christian faith does, however, make a claim that might seem to place the nature of God within the scope of historical statements when it claims that God was or became incarnate in Jesus. Whether it is in fact a historical statement and in what sense may depend in large measure on what we understand by "incarnate" here. For one can find a very wide range of ways of understanding this claim, extending from something like "God is involved in human life" or "God was involved in a particular and especially powerful and effective way in Jesus" to the full-blown definition of the Council of Chalcedon in 451: Jesus was and is

> at once complete in Godhead and complete in manhood, truly God and truly man, consisting also of a reasonable soul and body; of one substance with the Father as regards his Godhead,

The Nature of God—An Unanswerable Question?

> and at the same time of one substance with us as regards his manhood; like us in all respects, apart from sin; as regards his Godhead, begotten of the Father before the ages, but yet as regards his manhood begotten, for us men and for our salvation, of Mary the Virgin, the God-bearer; one and the same Christ, Son, Lord, Only-begotten, recognized in two natures, without confusion, without change, without division, without separation; the distinction of natures being in no way annulled by the union, but rather the characteristics of each nature being preserved and coming together to form one person and subsistence, not as parted or separated into two persons, but one and the same Son and only-begotten God the Word, Lord Jesus Christ.

Between the one rather vague interpretation of what is involved when we speak of "incarnation" and the other, an alarmingly detailed one, lie a number of different possibilities. At the one extreme, it seems to be more a matter of the character of God as shown in the life of Jesus, at the other, a far more precise definition of Jesus' nature—which in its speaking of something that God was or became seems to imply that one is talking of God's nature or essence or even of a change in that nature that took place at a particular point of time. That is implicit in the talk of the begetting of Jesus, just as it is implicit in the Gospel of John's assertion that "the Word became flesh" (1:14).

Such a change is presumably also involved when a theologian such as Jürgen Moltmann today speaks of a "history of God," although such a phrase is in itself ambiguous: it could mean, say, our history governed, controlled, and determined by God, but we should more likely see in such a phrase a dynamic rather than a static view of God, a God who has a history. This God is not unchangeable, immutable, unaffected by events such as the crucifixion of Jesus. Yet if such an event is not just an event in the life of Jesus, but also an event in the history, the life, the existence of God, we are still left with the problem of saying how we can know anything about the truth of these events as events in the history of God. That the crucifixion was an event in the history of Jesus is clear enough, but Jesus' cry on the cross to the God who had deserted him might suggest that this was an event in which Jesus' God played no part, but was simply and distressingly absent. If, however, this impression is a mistaken one, could it not mean that, on the contrary, God was very much involved in this event?

The question then would be: how far can or should we speak of a "history of God" that is separate and distinguished from the history of our world? Or is God in fact very much "in" that history and it "in" God and perhaps no more so than at that very point where God seems most glaringly absent, even to Jesus himself, namely in the death of God's servant on the cross? Yet how should we conceive of the God in whom that history finds its place? And here the problem of suitable criteria returns. "Coherence" may be attainable in statements about God, but "correspondence" remains far more difficult.

The Cambridge theologian Don Cupitt and the "sea of faith" movement that he inspired treat God and beliefs about God as human constructions and then go on to speak of a "non-real" God. The role of human construction and imagination may be readily granted here, but does it follow that a "non-real" God (a phrase whose intelligibility and suitability others have questioned) is the outcome of this way of thinking? For human works of art are certainly the result of human construction and imagination, but in many cases they relate to the artist's perception of reality. It would be unwise, however, to speak of their *corresponding to* this reality, more fitting to refer to their being *a response to* this reality as the artist sees it. However, that implies another sort of judgment than that which one concerning correspondence would normally involve: the latter is usually a factual one, sometimes involving even mathematical precision; if we ask, for instance, whether the traditional view of the Last Supper as involving Jesus and his twelve closest followers, no more, no less, corresponds to those who were actually present then, that is a question calling for mathematical precision—if we could be sure who was and was not present. Assessing a work of art as a response to a perceived reality is, on the other hand, an aesthetic one, involving an inevitably subjective judgment, a judgment not only of the appropriateness of the response in question, but also of the reality to which it is a response. One example is the discussion of the use of different literary plots in historiographical writing. For the question arose whether all forms of literary plot were valid and appropriate in handling a particular historical subject. Was "comedy," for instance, a possible choice when dealing with the Holocaust? To decide that one would need to bear in mind both the character of such a historical narrative and the character of the sequence of events that is being so described. (It may at first sight seem grotesque to suggest that possibility, but the discussion among philosophers of history, e.g., over the American cartoonist Art Spiegelmann's *Maus: A Survivor's Tale*, and the appearance of various works in other media indicate that there is room for debate here.) In the case of statements about God the nature of the reality that would be referred to by this word is a question to which we must return in the final chapter of this short work.

However, it may not only be in relation to statements that connect God and the historical life of Jesus that there will be a decided element of the aesthetic in these judgments. For, given the difficulty of recognizing "correspondences" between our world and God, such that we can confidently say that God must have been in this or that event or God must have done this or that, it may well be that the nearest we can come to such judgments may be more aesthetic in nature. We may, for instance, discern a certain "fit" between some events in the world and what we believe about God, a "fit" such that the absence of God leaves our understanding and appreciation of the world the poorer. This is no "God of the gaps," however, but rather an overall view of the world that recognizes in it certain patterns and regularities that may point to the existence and activity of a mysterious reality beyond and behind the visible and observable phenomena of our world. They may point in that way, but need not do so. If they do, that may be reckoned an aesthetic "plus." The precise nature of this mysterious reality will doubtless remain veiled in obscurity, but our tentative testimony to its presence may be regarded as our response to what we see in the world around us, a response that seems to have been part and parcel of humanity's perception of and response to our world from earliest times.

THREE

The Nature of God in Christian Tradition

Jesus' message, we saw, presupposed many of the views of God's nature that were embedded in Israel's traditions, and it had to be so in order to be intelligible; that was also essential if Jesus were to make plain what he was now claiming to be God's message. The points of contact with his ancestral traditions had to be clear if his message was to be seen as God's message and a message about this God. Even to recognize what was distinctive about Jesus' message presupposed an awareness of, and familiarity with, what was the usual and traditional view and what were the already existing varieties in those traditions. However, the stream of tradition did not stop there, but flowed on in the movement that came into being after Jesus' death and the experiences that his followers interpreted as his being raised from the dead. After a while they would speak of and to Jesus in terms appropriate to God, and in Jewish eyes in terms appropriate to God *alone*. That inevitably raised the question whether the

The God of Jesus—Our God?

Christian church had abandoned the monotheism of its Jewish roots and in fact now believed in two gods. The early Christians were unwilling to concede that this was the case and eventually there arose the doctrine of the Trinity, of the Christian God as three-in-one, the divine Spirit being added to Jesus and his Father.

God as Trinity?

It is true that this threesome was foreshadowed in the New Testament when all three are mentioned as if they belonged together and were to be set on the same level, as it were (e.g., Matt 28:19, in the risen Jesus' commission to his disciples; 2 Cor 13:13, in the closing benediction of the letter). There had been some preparation for this in the texts of the New Testament whose writings speak clearly of three entities (if we may call them that) that are somehow to be brought into relation with one another. For the earthly Jesus claims to act in the name of God, the God of his people Israel, whom he addresses as "father." And then there is that spirit that in John's Gospel is sent both by the Father (John 14:16, 26) and the Son (15:26) and that is described as another "Paraclete" (however one may think fit to translate that term, which probably refers to someone called to take their place alongside another, particularly as an advocate acting on their behalf in a court of law), taking up the role of the earthly Jesus after his departure (14:16). The risen Jesus bestows this spirit upon his disciples in order that they may continue his mission with the effect of moving their hearers to seek forgiveness or be condemned. It is true that the relationship of this spirit to Father and Son is less precisely described in the rest of the New Testament: for instance, Paul speaks at one moment of the spirit of God, at the next of the spirit of Christ, and then of the spirit of the one that raised Jesus from the dead (Rom 8:9–11). Despite that, the spirit that is meant here seems to be identified fully neither with God nor Christ.

Later theological formulations would describe all three as "persons," although there is today the danger that this word could be understood anachronistically in a modern, more psychological, sense. Originally the Latin word "*persona*" was used of the masks worn by actors to indicate the parts that they played on the stage. (Its Greek equivalent was the usual word for "face.") The suggestion then lies near at hand that these "persons" refer to the different roles played by the one God in relationship to humanity and the world (or in more technical, but certainly not more readily intelligible, language, the Roman Catholic theologian Karl Rahner's "manners of subsistence"), now as the mysterious other, now as the one who comes into the world as God's human message, now as the invisible presence of this God pervading and influencing the world and humanity.

The term could, however, easily be understood in a more modern sense in the case of Jesus and his Father as they spoke to one another and related to one another, as any two human persons might, but the reference to the spirit is more difficult; it has been suggested that John's Gospel may have given some impetus to this development, this expansion to embrace a third entity, when it speaks of the spirit coming in order to play a role in Jesus' followers' lives comparable to that of Jesus himself as long

The God of Jesus—Our God?

as he was still amongst them. It is, then, nonetheless surprising that God's spirit is found mentioned in this way in so early a text as 2 Corinthians, in the benediction of 13:13, considerably earlier than John's Gospel. This, however, may be deceptive; it is clear that gifts of the spirit of God and achieving fellowship despite divisive claims to spiritual endowment on the part of some members in that particular congregation were problems that are especially evident in 1 Corinthians, and these problems may well have influenced Paul in composing 2 Corinthians. Jesus' "grace" and God's "love" may reflect the disposition of these two towards the Corinthian Christians, but "fellowship" and "spirit" do not seem to be quite the same sort of thing. Does Paul, then, wish for them a fellowship, a oneness, "in" or produced by the spirit of God (rather than the "of" so predominant in English translations; but cf., e.g., the New English Bible, "fellowship in the Holy Spirit," J. B. Phillips' translation "the fellowship that is ours in the Holy Spirit," or the Common English Version's "may the Holy Spirit join all your hearts together")?

At any rate, whatever Paul's reasons for blessing the Corinthians in this way, in later Christian tradition the threefold nature of God remained; indeed, alongside those formulating the doctrine of the Trinity in the conventional way, there are Christian theologians who insist on the threefoldness while at the same time giving other names and identities to one or more of the three, as if there were an inescapable logic and necessity in this threefoldness. Whether the Father becomes "the Other" or something else, or the Son the world, the number three remains unchallenged. Indeed, it seems that in more recent times it is the presence of God's spirit and its right to be present that has caused fewer reformulations of the doctrine than the presence of the first two "persons."

However, the claim that this threeness is non-negotiable needs some examination. Not only is there the protest of the other monotheistic faiths, both Islam and Judaism, the latter of which was, after all, the faith of Jesus, but when a respected Christian theologian such as Geoffrey Lampe writes a book with the title *God as Spirit*, then the implication seems to be, and is, in Lampe's view, that one should not make a third, separate "person" out of the spirit or thus distinguish between the first and third "persons" of the Trinity. That leaves us then with God and with Jesus. But should both of these be considered to be "God"?

Jesus as God?

The word "Christ," which his followers went on to apply to Jesus, initially represented a title and only later came to be appropriated by them as his proper name. As a title it designated God's "anointed one," the Messiah. This figure was variously conceived, but even when a messianic figure came from heaven it was not viewed as God, but as God's emissary and messenger. It is clear from the Jesus-traditions that the question whether Jesus could be this "anointed one" sent by God was in the air at the time, and in view of the things that he did and the way that he spoke in God's name such a question was probably inevitable. Whether Jesus himself posed it, to himself or to others, and how he answered it may be less certain. The focus of his interest and concern was God, God's work, and

God's message, and he was certain of his responsibility to be the instrument of that work and the spreading of that message.

Before one overestimates the significance of this role in assessing Jesus' relationship to God it would be as well to note what some have called a "democratization" of the messianic role in Jesus' preaching, a "collective" understanding of that role. By that it is meant that Jesus took up themes and tasks that in Jewish expectations were variously attributed to an individual figure, the Messiah, and invited and called his immediate followers to share those tasks with him. We have in the gospel traditions accounts of Jesus commissioning disciples, either twelve or seventy(-two), to carry on his work, making it known and available to a wider circle (cf. Mark 6:7–13; Luke 10:1–12). In the future, too, the smaller group of disciples was evidently destined for the kingly role of judgment, sitting on thrones to judge Israel (Matt 19:28/Luke 22:30). In Luke 12:32 Jesus again seems to promise his disciples kingly rule: "Fear not, little flock! For it is your Father's will to give you the kingdom." That would be even clearer in Luke 22:29, "And I confer a kingdom on you just as my Father has conferred a kingdom on me," although one might question how far Jesus actually would have felt that he had the authority to confer such a kingdom. Even if this is a later formulation, the idea of the kingly rule of the disciples is clear. For it is to be noted that when a kingdom is given to someone that person exercises the role of a ruler. That can be seen in Daniel 7:27, "The kingdom and dominion and the greatness of the kingdoms under the whole heaven shall be given to the people of the holy ones of the Most High; their kingdom shall be an everlasting kingdom, and all dominions shall serve and obey them" (New Revised Standard Version). Does that apply as well to the promise given to the poor in the beatitude of Luke 6:20, where the kingdom is promised to the poor? While we may more often think of this as allowing them to enter into God's kingdom or to share in the good things that the kingdom brings, the doxology of the Lord's Prayer that has later been added to that prayer uses a similar phrase, "Thine is the kingdom" (Matt 6:13 according to some witnesses); that hardly refers to God's entry into the kingdom or sharing in its good things, but rather to God's kingly rule. What is then to prevent us from interpreting the promise to the poor as also meaning that they will share in exercising God's kingly rule, a reversal of their present position of weakness? This promise also seems to apply to children according to Mark 10:14 (cf. Matt 19:14; Luke 18:16): "Allow the children to come to me and do not prevent them; for to such as these God's kingdom belongs." And such a ruling in the eschatological kingdom of God would in those days without doubt be seen as a function of the Messiah.

Thus, when Jesus sees God's finger at work in his driving out of demons (Luke 11:20; Matt 12:28 has "spirit" instead of "finger"), that does not mean that that finger is not at work in the exorcisms practiced by others, including Jesus' disciples and especially in those performed by them. For it was in the works performed by them that Jesus saw the downfall of Satan (Luke 10:18). (That holds good if in fact the context in which Luke places the saying is the original one; for if, on the contrary, it was uttered by Jesus either with regard to some visionary experience of his own—e.g., at his baptism—or in connection with one of his own exorcisms, then this tells us nothing about his evaluation of the exorcisms performed by his followers. Nonetheless, it would then be surprising that Luke has chosen to put it in this context.)

In all these texts, it is striking that they do not exalt Jesus to a position above the whole of the rest of humanity, let alone above human existence itself, and that is a strong argument for the trustworthiness of this tradition. To this line of argument should be added the common fate and lot that Jesus shared with his disciples: they share his homelessness (Luke 9:58/Matt 8:20) and his renunciation of life in his family, and must reckon with sharing his suffering by bearing their own cross (Luke 14:27/Matt 10:38; cf. Mark 8:34/Matt 16:24/Luke 9:23). Jesus' question to the two sons of Zebedee, after their mother had begged him to grant them a place on his left hand and on his right in his glory, points in the same direction: "Can you drink the cup that I drink or be baptized with the baptism with which I am being baptized?" (Mark 10:38; cf. Matt 20:22). And lastly there are Jesus' actions during his last meal with his disciples, in his breaking and distributing bread and giving them the cup to drink; should one not understand them as, at the very least, actions that were meant to bind the disciples together with himself as he faced up to his imminent fate?

Quite obviously, sharing these tasks and roles with Jesus did not mean that his disciples were also taken up into the person of God. It does then become more difficult to speak of Jesus' uniqueness, the more he shares his status with his disciples and offers to share with them his way and indeed calls upon them to do so. There remains ultimately the fact that it is he who shares and offers all

The Nature of God in Christian Tradition

this in God's name, who made it possible then and still makes it possible. To do that, however, he does not need to be divine, but simply God's servant and messenger.

The same is true of Jesus' death: what at least the first three gospels describe is most naturally understood as the account of a man who believed himself to be God's messenger and, albeit reluctantly, takes upon himself in his prayers in Gethsemane the suffering that he sees as the consequence of his faithful obedience to an unpopular message, unpopular at least in the eyes of the civil and religious leaders of his day whom he confronts and challenges in Jerusalem. Whether he actually expected that suffering to be anything so unbearable and excruciating as crucifixion at the hands of the Romans is another matter, as is the question whether he was aware that God would not lift a finger to come to his rescue. At any rate, he reproaches God for leaving him to such a fate. Now there are some who argue that what is happening here can only be understood in terms of the doctrine of the Trinity, but their efforts to explain it in these terms seem instead to make the relations between Jesus and his God harder to comprehend. Placing the two together in the way that Trinitarian doctrine does makes it very hard to do justice to the distance between the two expressed in Jesus' cry on the cross.

Curiously, some who have insisted on a Trinitarian interpretation of the cross have also referred to a moving account in the book *Night*, written by Eli Wiesel, a survivor of Auschwitz and other camps, of the long drawn-out execution by hanging of a young Jew at Auschwitz: this prompted the onlookers to ask where God was, a question that in turn led Wiesel to say to himself that God was there, hanging on the gallows. That is a claim that comes very near to the bold and provocative language of a "crucified God," even if the mode of execution is different, and this raises the question how Jesus' death and, correspondingly, God's involvement in it and relationship to it differed from the death of the young Jew at Auschwitz. It is true that Jesus was identified with God's cause in a way and to a degree that was probably not true of the young Jew. (And the absence of such an identification with God's cause on the part of the young Jew precludes any attempt to claim that Trinitarian language or an ascription of divinity to him would be in the least appropriate here.) But can one go so far as to make this a qualitative difference as opposed to one of degree? Should we not recognize rather that it stands at one end of a spectrum that also embraces women and men who have suffered and been martyred for the sake of God's cause? It is claimed, then, that God suffers with them in their sufferings. On the other hand, there is no indication that the young Jew shared this insight into what he was enduring, but then neither, apparently, did Jesus, according to Matthew and Mark's accounts. In his cry on the cross we look in vain for any awareness that God was there with him, sharing his suffering.

Jesus the Messenger of God

Such speculations about the divine nature that find expression in the Christian doctrine of the Trinity in fact find little support in Jesus' life and teaching. There it is, rather, striking how much of that teaching speaks of

The Nature of God in Christian Tradition

Israel's God and the rule or kingdom of God in the form of parables. There it is a matter of the character of God and God's dealings with humanity, the nature of God in that sense, God's characteristic ways of dealing with the human world, and this character is only spoken of indirectly as the hearers are asked to enter into the often implicitly challenging situations portrayed in these stories. At least in part the indirectness involved here may stem from the reverent reluctance among Jews of that time to speak directly of God, preferring to use circumlocutions for God, of which "God's kingly rule" would be one example, meaning in effect God ruling as king. This rule was to be experienced in Jesus' ministry, above all in his healings (cf. Luke 11:20/Matt 12:28) and in his fellowship with the outcasts of Jewish society, and the experience found its interpretation above all in these stories that Jesus told. He did not define God for them, but rather pointed to what was going on around him and his hearers and said in effect, "There is God at work." When one saw this or that happening, then one knew that God was present and active. At the same time the element of the surprising, absurd, extravagant, or offensive that often occurs in Jesus' stories points to the way in which God's working surpasses anything that we can adequately comprehend from human experience.

These stories, drawing on human and interpersonal experience, often point to a God whose character and actions are set in relation either to surprising human actions and experiences or to the actions of human beings whose fitness to point to the character of God is at first sight by no means evident. For Jesus' hearers would not, for instance, expect that, when one of the despised tax-collectors and a member of the religiously zealous movement of the Pharisees went up to the Jerusalem temple to pray, it would be the former who left the place justified in God's eyes rather than the latter (Luke 18:9–14). Nor was it to be expected that the host at a great banquet would replace the invited guests who had declined his invitation with those who were poor, crippled, blind, and lame (Luke 14:16–24). The eagerness of a father to forgive his wayward son (Luke 15:11–32) was surprising for the son and perhaps for some of Jesus' audience too; at any rate the son had made his own proposal that might have seemed more just and appropriate, namely to be allowed to return with the same status as the day-laborers working for his father. Or there was the shocking decision of the vineyard owner to pay the same wage to all who had worked for him, whether they had done so for a whole day or just one hour (Matt 20:1–16). As a guide to the behavior of God this must have seemed shocking and abhorrent. Similarly disconcerting was the comparison between God and an unjust judge (Luke 18:1–8) or Jesus' apparent approval of the behavior of a dishonest administrator (Luke 16:1–12). And the story of the Samaritan in Luke 10:30–37 showed that members of that people, so despised by the Jews, could fulfill God's will better than members of God's own people, even ones going about their religious duties, who in all probability failed to do God's will because they were more concerned with their ritual purity.

Even when it is a matter of arguments and teaching based on ordinary, everyday life, Jesus' stories contain an element of surprise and even subversion, at least in the eyes of his critics. That a shepherd should go to look for a lost sheep would occasion no surprise, even if it might

The Nature of God in Christian Tradition

raise questions about the safety of the remainder of the flock, and a poor woman's thorough search for a lost coin would seem natural (Luke 15:4–10). What was surprising and potentially shocking was Jesus' use of such stories to justify the welcome that he himself extended to sinners and outcasts in God's name. Again, the revenge meted out by the vineyard owner to the evil tenants of the vineyard after they had put his son to death would have seemed a just punishment for their wickedness (Mark 12:9/Matt 21:41/Luke 20:16); the sting lay in the way that the story was turned against God's chosen people and its leaders. The natural world, too, yielded material with challenging consequences for Jesus' hearers: God's feeding the birds or ravens (Luke) and "clothing" of the lilies and the grass (Matt 6:26–31/Luke 12:22–29) called for a corresponding trust on the part of Jesus' human hearers. That God let the sun shine on good and evil and sent rain to just and unjust meant that Jesus' followers should accordingly love their enemies (Matt 5:44–47; cf. Luke 6:27–28), thus undermining any principles of reward and retribution—all could enjoy God's goodness.

That Jesus lived and taught within the context of traditions about God current amongst his people is clear, as we saw earlier, but it needs to be stressed that these traditions were not taken over uncritically. On the contrary, Jesus often pointed in his teaching and above all in his stories to a God who acted very differently and with very different principles to those traditionally expected of the divine dealings with humanity. And Jesus does not attempt to justify his different perception of God's character, and certainly not by means of doctrinal or philosophical arguments; he does not even say he is directly challenging these prevalent expectations and views, but simply lets his stories do their work. Even if one can see allusive hints at his own role in God's work, even in the son whom the vineyard tenants kill, that role need be no other than that of God's final messenger who brings to his fellow human beings the message that they are God's beloved children, a message he himself embraces to the full in his awareness of being one of these children. At the same time, as bearer of this message of this relationship with its revolutionary consequences for human conduct and human beings' relationship with God, he is aware of the special status that he enjoys as bringer of this message as the kingly rule of this fatherly God breaks into the world and is realized in the actions of his own ministry.

FOUR

And Our God?

With this question we return to that aspect of the book's title that may have surprised and even offended some. It was argued that it was a legitimate question to raise, but at this point one should be warned that it is a question that in turn begets further questions, and may end up with an answer that is but a further question or else the "learned (or not so learned?) ignorance" of which Nicholas of Cusa spoke. Despite all that we have since discovered about our world and ourselves, we may not have progressed much further since his day.

We saw that the question of the "nature" of God that was of concern to Jesus was a matter of the divine *character*, not the existence of God. That existence he assumed, as did his Jewish contemporaries, and many of their assumptions about the God of Israel were ones he fully shared. The questions raised by philosophers both before his time as well as later and the reflections of Christian theologians did not trouble him. In other words, many of our questions will find no help in Jesus' teaching and for some that might be a sign that we should leave those questions alone. Yet they do trouble us and should do so, for we cannot with integrity and a good conscience cast aside two millennia of intellectual history and questioning and simply revert to the ways of thinking of Palestine in the first century.

One solution has been to deny that Jesus was really talking about, or needed to talk about, God at all. What seem at first sight to be theological statements or assertions about God are in reality anthropological statements, statements about human existence. Talk of serving God should be rephrased to become talk of serving our fellow human beings, our human neighbors, thus reducing Jesus' double command to love God and one's neighbor (Mark 12:28–34/Matt 22:36–40; cf. Luke 10:27) to the single command to love that neighbor. When one asks where God's grace and forgiveness find a place in this, the answer is found (according to Herbert Braun, a pupil of Rudolf Bultmann, that theologian and philosopher who exercised so great an influence on the theology of the twentieth century) in one's acceptance by one's human fellows and above all by oneself. Such an existential exposition of Jesus' message is doubtless possible as a reinterpretation of that message, but it must be recognized that it hardly corresponds to Jesus' own self-understanding or the course of his life. And whether it would be right to claim he accepted himself is hard to say; at any rate the destiny he felt God had in store for him is one he found difficulty in accepting, as the accounts of Gethsemane and Golgotha show. And only some of his neighbors accepted him, but proportionally very few of them.

And Our God?

So, if God played a vitally important part in Jesus' thinking and teaching, yet we cannot simply take his God for our own, what are we to do? Two possible paths to finding our own view of God are to be found, some claim, firstly in the nature of the physical world in which we live, and secondly in religious experience. It needs to be asked how true that is and then what part Jesus and his belief in God could and would play in the resultant beliefs or, if neither path proves satisfactory, whether Jesus and his beliefs can still offer us something.

God and the Universe

It used to be the case that the "argument from design" played an important part in arguments for God's existence, along with such philosophically based arguments as the related cosmological argument that there must be a first cause for all that exists, for the existence of the universe that manifests this design, and the ontological argument that says, put crudely, that which can be conceived of must exist (for, in the last analysis, the classic argument of the medieval theologian Anselm of Canterbury seems to rest on some such assumption, his argument namely that because we can conceive of God as a perfect being, as one whom no greater can be conceived, then God exists, not just in our minds but also as a reality outside our minds—a principle that also appears to offer some considerable scope for science fiction and things like artists' portrayals of hell or heaven). Alongside this trilogy of arguments we also find a moral argument that there must be a moral God for there to be moral laws (which there

The God of Jesus—Our God?

are). The "argument from design" (or often, more accurately, "the argument *to* design") is a line of argument that is still advanced by some. For many wonder at the mysteries and the regularities of the natural world in which we live, many of them natural scientists too, although perhaps few today would endorse without qualification the claim made by Joseph Addison at the beginning of the eighteenth century (a claim that seems to echo the ancient Pythagoreans and their "music of the spheres"):

> What though in solemn silence all
> Move round the dark terrestrial ball?
> What though no real voice nor sound
> Amid the radiant orbs be found?
> In reason's ear they all rejoice,
> And utter forth a glorious voice,
> Forever singing as they shine,
> "The hand that made us is divine."

So direct a path to knowledge of God's existence and the work of creation may be illusory, although it certainly still has its supporters in some circles. Nonetheless, one could claim that the mind-boggling immensities in time and space to which modern astronomy and physics point us, as well as the subtle complexities pervading our world, down to the tiniest particles that make up the reality of our physical world, and the puzzles and mysteries with which time and space still present us, have all contributed to a heightened and deepened sense of wonder at this physical mystery in which we live, even if not all would trace this back to a personal God or indeed to any God at all. It is to be noted, however, that such aesthetic arguments are to be distinguished from the use of such arguments mentioned at the end of the second chapter. Here

And Our God?

there is the temptation to infer from the wonders of the natural world the existence of an artist, personal or impersonal, a creative force that has brought these wonders into being. That is different to judging statements about God aesthetically with a view to their appropriateness as a response to a given reality, in this case those wonders of the natural world just referred to, although aesthetic arguments may be involved at both levels. If the regularities of the natural world gave rise to the picture of God as a divine watchmaker that sets the machinery of the world in motion (so the eighteenth-century English deist William Paley), aesthetic judgments may well reject that picture as inappropriate both to what we know of the natural world and what we otherwise want to assert about God, indeed as a rather crude picture of God and God's relation to the world.

Frequently we find that the personal creator is replaced by something like a "big bang" (a secular version of the "first cause" of philosophical theology?), a mysterious and breath-takingly brief event at the beginning of time and of the existence of the universe. The alternative to such a beginning would be a cyclic view in which the matter of the universe always exists, takes shape, eventually collapses in on itself, and then begins again—a view reminiscent of the ancient Stoic philosophers with their succession of conflagrations in which the world was destroyed, only to begin all over again (although perhaps one does not also need to postulate that each new beginning takes exactly the same form as its predecessors, so that, for example, this author or his look-alike would be sitting there in x million years writing it all again). Is it that the more fashionable "big bang" theory concentrates purely on our present universe and ignores any other universes that may have preceded it prior to their imploding? Whichever of these possibilities we choose, the single "big bang" or a continuous succession of new beginnings (and there may be other possibilities), it is to be noted that the natural sciences will have explained the "how?" of this beginning and of the subsequent history of the universe, but not the "why?" Perhaps, if the cyclic view was true, one might be spared the "why?" question and could simply reply that it always has been so and always will be so. If, however, we opt for the single "big bang" we are faced with further questions: if it was effective was it, so to speak, the very first attempt to light the fuse (who put a flame to the blue paper or are we to think more properly of some sort of self-combustion)? Or was it but one of a finite or even infinite number of attempts at such a self-combustion that had all fizzled out, but which, had another one of them also been successful, would have produced a universe different from the one in which we find ourselves? And it is when one weighs up the statistical probability or rather improbability of such a course of events taking place spontaneously that doubts creep in about the plausibility of such a fully fortuitous happening. For the theory of a "big bang" without some guiding or prompting force at work behind it seems, if anything, more mysterious than a theory that postulates such a force. It might seem simpler, if one wanted a cosmogony or cosmology without divine intervention, to opt rather for some version of a perpetual cycle of explosions and implosions.

It must be recognized that scientific explanations impress us by their ability to explain the complex concat-

And Our God?

enations of cause and effect that shape the world in which we live. They are, moreover, able to predict that if X happens Y will follow, if other factors do not prevent it. This ability to explain and predict is based on observations of the present (or what we can observe in the present if we take into account that events in outer space may have actually taken place long before our observable evidence reaches us). When it comes to speaking of the pre-history of what we see before us an element of the hypothetical and imaginative enters in as we seek to reconstruct, with help of various models and formulae borrowed from the present, what might have happened in the past. This element of the hypothetical and imaginative has much in common with the quality of aesthetic judgments discussed earlier, as we attempt to sketch a scenario that fits what we know of the world and its workings today.

The "argument from design" being considered here, in speaking of "design" seems, perhaps, implicitly to have introduced the idea of a designer and thereby some sort of personal element, even if one does not embellish the "design" with adjectives like "intelligent" or "intentional"; and some might want to question the intelligence of some of the design or the morality of the intentions. Rather, one should speak of regularities or patterns, as when we see certain cloud formations or the undulations left by the tide on a beach. Both these patterns can be physically explained and one could argue the same for the multitude of patterns recognizable in our physical world. It is only when we push back behind the physical explanations to the reason why these themselves exist, not treating them as if they were in the last analysis necessary or self-evident, that we come up against the "why?" question: *why* are there regularities and why precisely *these* regularities? And it is here that the role of hypothesis and imagination is perhaps most clearly visible.

Again, the coming into being of *homo sapiens* is perhaps more tangible and explicable, although it is to be recognized that the paths and routes that the various species have in fact taken remain conjectural, perhaps none more so than the various stages that produced human beings as we know them today. There remain, at any rate, a number of aspects of human existence that, as we noted, seem to distinguish us, as far as we know, from the highest forms of animal life (self-reflection, self-criticism, and self-transcendence were the three mentioned above), and it is legitimate to wonder why we are blessed (if it is a blessing, for these can and do complicate our existence) with such characteristics. Theories of evolution of various sorts may take us a certain way in tracing the path by which we developed from our nearest animal ancestors, but explaining why we, for instance, walk upright rather than on all fours is a very different matter to explaining why we possess the characteristics just mentioned. One could account for them by appealing to the notion of humanity's being created in the image and likeness of God (Gen 1:26–27) or, if one wishes to avoid such a view of humanity's creation, one could instead postulate a continuing presence of something of the divine in human beings, a presence that many Christians would identify as the presence of the or a divine spirit.

In the past, such a spirit pervading humanity or indeed the whole world or universe was frequently regarded as something impersonal, a physical substance, even if not the most solid of them. Yet distinctions such

And Our God?

as "material" or "non-material" may be of little help to us today as we realize that the material, which used to be thought of as solid and substantial, is made up of tiny particles and electrical fields. On the other hand, the realization that holds good for us, too, may be a suggestive starting-point. There are many dimensions and aspects of that elusive concept, the human person, some of them perceived as physical, sometimes all too physical, others less overtly so, although we realize something of the role played by such things as electrical impulses in the human brain as facilitating and undergirding these aspects. Though some will speak of a thoroughgoing physical determinism, many of us shy away from that, appealing to the experience of the exercise of the human will, human decisions, as well as those qualities of self-reflection and self-transcendence referred to before. Nevertheless we realize that our wills are not supreme here, being restrained by the limitations of our physical natures as well as those of our human brains. Injuries and illnesses can restrict the free exercise of our wills and our perceptions even more, even to the point where the person we once were is no longer recognizable, where the person who once was no longer even knows who he or she is, let alone being aware of those interpersonal relationships that were so important for his or her personhood. Yet, as long as all still functions, at least to some degree, we experience ourselves as persons (and will feel much aggrieved if we feel that our worth as persons is being denied by others), while being uncertain what constitutes this personhood. It may be made up of a number of things, with memory playing an important part, but also relationships with others and so forth, and physical factors playing their part here too, as we realize, for instance, when injury to the brain impairs the memory.

In speaking of "persons," and also when we speak of the "self," which could correspond to the "person" seen from the inside, as it were, we use a term that implies a whole range of things—the physical, the psychological, as well as the capacity to be more or less aware of this whole complex of these different aspects and dimensions of the person. The person or the self is not, however, "in" any parts of this complex nor can it really be said to be "in" the whole of it as one used to speak of the human soul. On the other hand, it is possible to speak of an individual's personality, that is, the character of the person in question, permeating or pervading the whole of her or his being, and this way of speaking may be more fruitful for us at this point, as we shall later see. Nor can it be said to be "outside" or "other than" this complex, nor even "above" it despite its seemingly self-transcendent powers. One way of speaking of it might be to call it a "construct," as human self-analysis has set together more and more complementary aspects and dimensions that go to make up what we experience as personhood and selfhood. Yet again, though, it needs to be noted that the fact that we have "constructed" this concept does nothing to call in question the reality of that which we have constructed, a construction that is permanently open to empirical testing and reappraising self-analysis.

Without invoking concepts such as that of a "world-soul," it is still possible to ask whether this microcosmic analogy is to some degree suggestive when applied to the world in which we live. If it is suggested, as we saw earlier, that God is to be seen as a human construction, we also saw that the analogy with works of art warned us against denying the reality of what had been thus constructed, although allowing for the presence of a degree of subjectivity that is inevitably part of an aesthetic judgment such as this would be. There is doubtless an element of subjectivity when dealing with some aspects of the human person, although others seem to offer the hope of empirical exactitude. For exact scientific examination of parts of the human being is possible and becomes ever more possible, even when the application of similar precision to other aspects such as the psychological is more limited, an important restriction when one considers, for instance, the role of memory in the awareness of selfhood. When the whole universe is involved, however, it is a very different matter indeed, where clinical trials on a macrocosmic scale are out of the question and much of the theorizing is largely hypothetical and abstract.

In some circles a form of belief in God known as "panentheism" ("all *in* God," as opposed to the "all *is* God" of "pantheism") is popular, and this would offer an analogy with the concept of the person or the self as a (human) construct embracing a whole complex of aspects and dimensions of the universe as we experience it; a far vaster complex, naturally, than that which is involved when we are considering only the human individual. To talk of all or everything being "*in* God" may strike us as odd, although it should be recalled that the author of the Acts of the Apostles puts on the lips of the apostle Paul as he preaches before the philosophers of Athens a statement that God is the one in whom all people "live and move and have their being" (Acts 17:28). Encouraged by the following reference to "some" of the Greek poets this

The God of Jesus—Our God?

is usually recognized as a quotation from the poet Aratus who wrote in the third century before the Christian era and was influenced by Stoic thought. That we are here said to be "in" this being is the more noteworthy in that the Stoics also spoke, and that more frequently, of the divine or the divine spirit in us. Yet it is one thing to speak of humanity being in God, of its being God's offspring as Paul goes on to say, quite another to speak of the entire cosmos in God. And yet, with their view of a divine rationality pervading, holding together, and shaping the physical world, it seems that on this level, too, these ancient thinkers could hold together as complementary ideas of the cosmos in God and God in the cosmos—not only "all in God," but also "God in all" (yet to my knowledge "theenpantism" has, fortunately, not been added to the galaxy of -isms that beset theological and philosophical discourse).

There is, we may note, a curious and enigmatic parallel to this "in" language in the apocryphal Coptic *Gospel of Thomas* where Jesus states: "I am the light that is over all things. I am all: from me all came forth, and to me all attained. Split a piece of wood; I am there. Lift up the stone, and you will find me there" (logion 77, translated by S. Patterson and M. Meyer). It is fashionable in some circles to value this later work highly as a witness to the teaching of Jesus, and undoubtedly some of the sayings in it bear comparison with their parallels in the first three gospels, but it is hard to convince oneself that this particular saying came from Jesus' lips. Nor did he seem to have said anything comparable about his heavenly father. Meyer is probably nearer the mark in comparing a passage from the second-century Greco-Roman writer, Lucian

And Our God?

of Samosata (*Hermotimus* 81, "God is not in heaven but rather permeates all things, such as pieces of wood and stones and animals, even the most insignificant"), which would suggest that the idea has been borrowed from popular philosophy.

However, the spatial imagery of the "in," used both by ancient writers and by more recent philosophers and theologians (what is known as "process theology" springs to mind) may be misleading here; it may be better to speak of a mutual interaction between this "other" force and the world, a world that of course includes human beings. It may also be advisable to avoid making this interaction in any way one-sided so that the one is wholly dependent on, and affected by, the other. And particularly when one will do justice to the relationship between the suffering Jesus and this "other" as well as to that between this "other" and a world that is, at least as far as we can assess it, marked by suffering and imperfection, then it is better to speak of this "other" as sharing in this suffering, be it that of Jesus or of the world at large.

We, too, can speak of a rationality pervading the universe, detectable in the regularities that we observe there and the often formulaic, mathematical, and algebraic expressions of these regularities. And yet, tempting as it may be to claim "God as spirit" as the reason for these regularities, it is important to remember how far from personal such a God would be, and also how potentially deterministic such a rule of reason would be. True, a God in the grip of ineluctable rules cannot be blamed for the evils of our world, but does such a slave of rules and laws deserve the name "God"? Nor, if there is any analogy to be found here in our own experience of our own human natures, would we want to speak of being so enslaved to our physical constitution that we are unable to change or guide anything by our own decisions. Perhaps the ancient Stoics may have been fatalistic in their thinking about their individual lives, despite their stress on divine reason as spirit indwelling human beings (the early Stoic teacher Cleanthes prays that the supreme God Zeus and fate may lead him wherever it has long been determined, and he will follow their leading, but even should he not want to it would make no difference—quoted in Seneca, *Enchiridion* 53), but it does not follow that we should copy them in this. And if we treat the enquiry about God in relation to the cosmos and ourselves as of the nature of an aesthetic judgment, then there should be no suggestion that we are offering a thoroughgoing empirical description of the physical nature of the world as it is or of ourselves as we are. Natural scientists, too, as we have seen, must ultimately content themselves with hypotheses and models and we should certainly not claim to be able to do any better. Indeed, at first sight we may seem to be worse off, further removed from reality or critical evaluation, when we invoke the comparison with works of art and their standing in relation to reality.

The analogy with works of art raises the question, however, of the appropriateness of the aesthetic judgment or judgments implied. For a work of art can tell us as much about the artist as it does about the reality portrayed, and appreciation of the work is likely to depend on how our experience of that which is depicted coincides with, or is at least sympathetic to, that of the artist. Yet there, too, the analogy may hold good: how often do portrayals of the divine reflect the experience of the world of the human worshippers that have fashioned that portrayal. In short, it is a question of the nature of the religious experience of the people in question or at least of their judgment of the experience that they designate as "religious."

God and Us

Our experience of the natural world may often take on a worship-like wonder and awe, although our experience may also often be one of horror, despair, and resentment, even though humanity may sometimes be largely to blame for what the natural world can inflict upon us. Our experience of the world may therefore only sometimes be "religious" in a positive sense, for at times the natural forces and their manifestations to which we are exposed may seem nearer to the demonic. If our "religion" is dualistic that may be no problem: both the positive and the negative experiences may then be "religious." On the other hand, if God is to be "good," then a considerable selectivity will be necessary in what we consider a "religious" experience, an experience, say, that philosopher of religion Rudolf Otto described as the "numinous." Only a part, indeed probably a very small part, of our experience of the world will qualify as "religious," like small peepholes offering a glimpse of a reality lying beyond the world.

But what of the individual's experience that is the context for such judgments and that shapes the form that they take? For that is surely bound up with the inclination to find a "religious" dimension in the world at large. That, too, will be selective, indeed forming the basis of the selectivity that we employ in deciding what are "religious" experiences in the world. An important part of this selection will be the social and religious context in which we each find ourselves: this involves society in general or the section of society in which we are placed, as well as the religious environment, if that is to be distinguished from society in general. In the case of Jesus, for instance, first-century Palestinian Jewish society was religiously shaped, although various groupings limited the homogeneity of this religious society. In addition it was confronted and dominated by a different religious society, that of the Greco-Roman Mediterranean world, and this coexistence led to countless tensions, culminating eventually in the first century in the Jewish revolt of 66.

Nevertheless there were important similarities: the belief in evil spirits and demons, for instance, was common to the larger Mediterranean culture and to the Jewish culture of Palestine. It is true the Jewish faith was more confident that its God had the upper hand and did and would triumph over these forces of evil, but a glance at the stories of Jesus' healing work in the first three gospels plainly shows how even in that Jewish world the belief in the presence and the exercise of power by these evil forces was commonplace. That is no longer true to the same extent, at least in Western culture, although even there such beliefs are unfortunately still to be found, and receive, even in some mainline churches, a certain undergirding in the liturgies and language used there. Nevertheless, this points to an important shift in the perception of God in relation to the world and humanity, a shift not only between Jesus' world and ours, but also between Jesus and us, for he clearly shared his world's belief in these evil forces, and regarded it as one of his tasks to subdue

And Our God?

these powers in God's name and to rescue his fellow human beings from the evil and suffering that were inflicted upon them. His success in resisting these powers was in his eyes, as we saw, a sign of the breaking into the world of God's kingly reign (Luke 11:20; cf. Matt 12:28).

It is important, however, to distinguish between a religious perspective that a particular individual chooses and one that is forced or imposed upon him or her to a greater or lesser extent. This view of the world as a battlefield between good and evil forces was a view that was part and parcel of the world into which Jesus and his contemporaries were born. That Jesus belonged to this world is indicated by his vision of Satan being dethroned as the disciples carried on Jesus' work of driving out evil spirits from the possessed (Luke 10:18). On the other hand, we have also noted that there were amongst Jews of that time different views about things like the nature of the world to come or the future existence of the individual or even the nature of God, and in such matters there was obviously room for choice of one perspective or another. The scope for too great an eclecticism would obviously be reduced, however, as soon as one opted to join one of the particular Jewish groupings current at that time. If one joined the movement of the Pharisees, for instance, one would be expected to believe in resurrection in some form or other.

It was, too, a world in which visions of the endtime and the world to come played a considerable role, whether the accounts of the visions are literary or, as was doubtless often the case, based on actual experiences in dreams and the like. Jesus was also a visionary figure, as Luke 10:18, cited above, and other passages in the Jesus-traditions suggest. In his social context such experiences might well be expected of him if he were viewed as a prophet, and such experiences continued to play an important role in the early church as the letters of Paul clearly show. Such a direct contact with God and the heavenly world would not have occasioned surprise; the Greco-Roman world at large was used to such claims by ecstatic seers and others and did not immediately dismiss them as illusory; on the contrary, they were often treated with the greatest respect, along with the interpretation of omens and the inspection of the entrails of sacrificial victims, which were also expected to yield information about what was to come to pass.

Many such features of the religious culture of the ancient world we would today dismiss as outdated superstitions. Yet they were an important way in which the ancients believed themselves to be directly in contact with their God or gods. Still today there are those who lay claim to somewhat comparable experiences, but it is important to note the context in which they occur and are treated seriously. For no longer is there a worldwide acceptance of the possibility and credibility of claims to such experiences, but rather in certain religious groups, and there in a form shaped and conditioned by the beliefs of the group in question. It is, for instance, within the context of the Roman Catholic faith that we find an important role given to visions of the mother of Jesus and other saints. Within Protestant traditions in general visions play a lesser role, although here the claims of charismatic groups are to be noted. Visions may be experienced there, more likely of the exalted Jesus rather than his mother, but also experiences of speaking in other tongues, as attested above all in Acts 2 as well as 1 Corinthians 12 and 14, although the

And Our God?

accounts of the apostle and the author of Acts are notoriously hard to reconcile fully with one another. In particular they seem to be divided over the question whether those speaking in tongues speak intelligibly and therefore whether their utterances are of benefit to those who hear them. At any rate, at first sight these experiences seem to be evidence of direct contact between the heavenly world and ourselves.

Quite apart from these more specifically Christian experiences, others will appeal to the "paranormal," to phenomena dealt with under the heading of "parapsychology," that also involve visions and premonitions and telepathic communication and the like. Yet, rather than see these as somehow evidence of the divine or another world, it may be more appropriate to recognize them as evidence that human nature is more complex and has a wider range of dimensions of capacities and experiences than the more prosaically minded among us are given to think. Others have appealed to "near-death" experiences where someone is on the point of death and experiences something like a very bright light, but that again may say more about the complexity of human nature, at least in some cases. (My own such experience of a "near-death" was far less informative: I was simply unconscious.) Yet these supposed signs of, or contacts with, another world or a world awaiting us beyond the grave do not seem to provide us with the sure evidence we would like and need. They seem equally likely to show that this world and at least some of the human lives within it have dimensions that are not at first sight generally apparent. Nor can we cast back to the resurrection appearances of Jesus, since it is by no means clear what the nature of those appearances was. All that is clear is that his disciples came to believe that God had raised him from the dead; historically nothing is certain beyond that assertion. It is true that Paul regards life in this world, including that of Jesus and himself, as worthless if there is no resurrection to a new, heavenly life (1 Cor 15:14–19), but how many of us would want to deny any value to the lives of those two men and countless others if they were not going to be raised from the dead? Do we not in fact judge them in the light of their this-worldly lives and find there much to be admired, even if we remain critical on some points, a criticism that is, however, not going to be altered by their resurrection if we knew of it. That is all the more significant in view of the role that expectations about another world and an afterlife have played in the thinking, not only of Jesus and his contemporaries, but countless others, of many different faiths, before and after, up to the present day; such beliefs have weighed heavily upon human life in this world and have served to shape its ethics and morality, sometimes for the better, but more often for the worse. Would it not be better to contradict Paul and flatly state that we must live for this life in this world, for anything beyond this is pure speculation?

Nor do the claims for a specifically Christian "hot-line" to the divine inspire much more confidence. Is this evidence of a supernatural link with the divine realm any more sound than the evidence just mentioned? Is it, for a start, a link between that realm and all human beings, as the appeals to the sphere of parapsychology might suggest, or, in the case of the claims of Christian charismatics, only some, privileged or especially gifted persons? Is it a link that is there in us all, only needing to be activated (by God

And Our God?

or by us?). In that case it would be something like what the seventeenth-century Quaker George Fox described as "that of God," the light, in everyone. On the other hand, it has been treated, both in the first century and today, as something that sets some Christians apart from all the rest and marks out those who are truly Christians. That was so in Paul's church in Corinth, despite his pointing out that the divine spirit is manifested in many other ways, too, many of them more useful to the well-being of the community than speaking words that are unintelligible to the rest of its members. That is true today, both in the separate existence of Pentecostalist churches and in the relations between members of other denominations. At a time when the Church of Scotland was much exercised by the question of the evaluation of, and the role played by, such charismatic manifestations in congregations, it was reported that a group representing the charismatic movement had offered to meet with a doctrinal committee of that church and to speak in tongues and let the committee judge for itself what it thought of this phenomenon. There was, it seems, little hint of a working of the divine spirit that was under the sole control of God, despite the impression we get in the New Testament that it was and should be so. One has, instead, the impression of a human religious technique that can be employed at will by the human subject, comparable to the use of, say, a rosary or mantras, and which those using it find religiously helpful.

More traditional streams of Protestantism stress, instead, such features as music and above all the preaching of the "word of God." Different forms of music may undoubtedly be religiously uplifting and inspiring for different groups of people and that has probably been mostly true of the religious person from time immemorial (there are exceptions in groups that consider silence to be of the essence of religious experience). For many who lay great weight on the role of the "word of God" in their lives, particularly those who hold the Christian Bible to be directly inspired by God in a way that no other writing is, there is here a direct link to their God by which they are called and guided. "Inspiration" is, however, a term that can be used in a great many ways, and is so used, and by no means entails the consequence that God was actually directly and sovereignly dictating the content of the Scriptures, even if such views of prophetic inspiration were current in the Greco-Roman world. That is not our experience today, nor do we hear a voice from heaven speaking to us as God is alleged to have spoken, for instance at Jesus' baptism (Mark 1:11/Matt 3:17/Luke 3:22). What we do find in the writings of the Jewish and the Christian Bibles is a great variety of texts of varying antiquity, some of whose authors are known to us, while other writings remain anonymous; their form and content are very varied and it is far from clear that their message is always the same or that their assertions can easily be reconciled with one another. It is, accordingly, more appropriate to view them as the product of human witness and human experience of the divine or the supposedly divine. These diverse texts are a witness that are, on the one hand, to be evaluated critically, both in the context of the witness born in the rest of these writings and in the light of our own experience and reflection upon it; and, on the other hand, a witness that we may wish to take up and appropriate for ourselves, but most likely not in its entirety. Rather, we may wish to treat some parts of it as more central than others and as pointing more helpfully and clearly to what we hold to be valuable insights. One way of putting that, if it is not misunderstood, would be to say that a human word may become for us a word of God. In all this at any rate, the element of human interpretation and appropriation is clear and dominant.

Jesus, Jesus' God, and Us

So far the results of this study may have seemed depressingly negative. Neither the nature of the cosmos nor our human experience seem to offer a firm basis either for asserting the existence of God, of whatever sort, nor offer us clear insight into the divine nature. The cosmos might have come into being of its own accord (or, alternatively, might have always been there) and, if it points to any sort of being or mystery behind it, the nature of that being or mystery remains highly ambiguous and certainly not unambiguously benevolent (nor intelligent). And our human experience is similarly ambiguous. Certainly what some sense as tokens of the divine are not so perceived by others, and much that is claimed as evidence of an invisible (divine) world may be better understood as evidence of traits of human nature or the human nature of some that seem to elude the demands for hard empirical, clinical evidence and explanation.

Throughout this work, too, we have been confronted by two alternative approaches. The one takes as its starting-point certain philosophical and theological premises and attempts within this framework to find a place for the man Jesus and his words and actions in relation to God. The other takes the man Jesus—above all as witnessed in the first three gospels, interpreted critically—and asks what, if anything, the life of this man allows us to infer about the nature of God. The former approach, I have suggested, seems to beg too many questions, but the latter threatens to leave us with little to go by. For, on the one hand, we saw that Jesus' assumptions about God and the divine nature were heavily influenced by the ways of thinking of his contemporaries, and, perhaps even more seriously, the traditions about his passion and death opened up the possibility that he had both misunderstood what God's purposes for him were, and then died disillusioned because God had not seemingly fulfilled what he had expected. And that is, I suggest, of little comfort to those who seek in Jesus' life and teaching a model for their own lives and beliefs. And neither approach seems to operate with a view of God's nature with which either I or many others would feel either comfortable or satisfied.

Yet our comfort and satisfaction may be far from unimportant considerations if it is right to stress the nature of judgments on such matters as having the nature of aesthetic judgments. In other words, it is significant if we are uncomfortable with the idea that the cosmos in which we find ourselves is just a chance formation brought about by certain physical regularities that just happen to be operative. We may also do well to wonder whether the whole process of evolution has just happened to end up with *homo sapiens* as its end-result (or is there yet a further stage to which *homo sapiens* must yet evolve? There might certainly be reason to suppose that the wisdom implied in the *sapiens* could be improved). Is that *all* just a product of laws of natural selection? One may doubt that all the more if the German theologian Gerd Theissen is right to point to the operation of a "cultural evolution"

And Our God?

that operates with rules that seem at many points to be the opposite of those of natural or "biological" evolution: for, rather than leading to the survival of the fittest, such an evolution would care for and provide for the weak, at least if it is to be in accord with the message and life of Jesus. While biological evolution might interpret death as failure, a culture focusing on the dying Jesus is bound to assign death a new value and worth, particularly when it is, like his, a death of voluntary self-giving and obedience to his father's will, whether he rightly understood that will or not.

This sort of aesthetic judgment, we have seen, involves selectivity, and nowhere is this clearer than in a case like this, for it is not self-evident or predetermined that we should choose to value this sort of cultural evolution. Plenty of our fellow human beings most certainly do not, and favor instead a culture that resembles biological evolution in its striving for power at the cost of others. Nor is it clear that those rejecting such a quest for power and preferring the sort of cultural evolution just mentioned do so just because they are more enlightened or because it suits them. Certainly it may well not make their lives either easier or more comfortable. When asked why they choose this way they may appeal to morality or say that their consciences prompt them to follow a life and to seek a society of this sort. With this inner prompting have we returned to the idea of a God as spirit that as an unseen Other is the source of this moving and prompting? And yet it is clearly not a moving and prompting that forces us to follow its path, for countless rarely do so or perhaps even do not do so at all. Even for those of us who do respond to this prompting our response is usually not complete or full, for we often ignore this leading and guidance.

At this point it should be noted that, if we abandon the conception of a personal God modeled on our experience of human personality and opt instead for some sort of personal or impersonal force permeating the world and ourselves, then we need to make an important distinction between the relationship between this force and the human world and the non-human world. For, while it may impress us, as it impressed ancient philosophers and their successors, how this world is shaped by regularities and predictabilities that one could attribute to the control or prompting of some unseen force, when it comes to ourselves the matter is rather different. We may still speak of some unseen force (e.g., conscience) prompting us, less often of one controlling us, unless we enter the realm of mental disorders or that of lower-order processes within our physical constitution, which may operate both in the healthy body or in the diseased. The prompting force, as opposed to the controlling one, however, is one to which we must first respond if it is to be effective, and this makes it difficult to speak of a single force that permeates uniformly both the human and the non-human world. However many those analogies referred to earlier that we may see between the relation of God and the cosmos and God and ourselves may seem to be, or between our perception of God and our perception of our own selves, at this point they may lead us astray. The unseen Other may function in a similar way with regard to the physical regularities of the cosmos and those present in our physical natures, but when it comes to a certain level of awareness—conscience, self-awareness, moral decisions, and

And Our God?

the like—we have the feeling that it is up to us to decide and choose, and many would be reluctant to call that feeling an illusion. And yet, if we are asking about the nature of God or of some force that might merit the designation "divine," might one not suppose that this mysterious Other somehow embraces both dimensions, the order of our amazing cosmos and the moral promptings that we experience as human beings? Or does that assumption ignore the danger that we saw earlier, of supposing that we can know what this mystery is or is not?

We should recall again that we should not expect Jesus' view of God to help us in understanding God's nature in the sense of a definition (were any such thing possible). We saw that he basically shared the views of his Jewish contemporaries on this question, neither questioning nor needing to argue for the existence of God. His God too was a personal being, a superhuman figure modeled on, but greatly excelling, the powers of human plenipotentiaries. Where Jesus' teaching is instructive and often innovative and distinctive is rather in the matter of the character of God, so that, whatever image, if any, we have of God or a divine force, it is legitimate to ask how far that image and the human attitudes and conduct that flow from it conform to, and are shaped by, those features of Jesus' teaching. And if, in the last analysis, we remain undecided about the existence of God, let alone the divine nature, it is still worthwhile to ask how far the man Jesus, believing what he did about the character and will of God, shapes our worldview or should do so.

At any rate, in trying to make sense of our world, in trying to fit it into any framework of understanding, we must inevitably select certain features, a certain perspective, as pointing to the way ahead rather than others. This should not be seen as an arbitrary choice, but should rather be justified with arguments as far as possible. And yet the nature of those arguments, which I have compared to aesthetic arguments, may seem to lay us open to the charge of arbitrariness and subjectivity, even if in the last analysis one must make a choice. The choice we make and the viewpoint we adopt must, at any rate, take into account both (a) our experience of the natural world and our intersubjective social experience and (b) our self-perception and self-awareness. How does Jesus' teaching about God contribute anything to this? Can we find clues in that teaching even if we must remain skeptical about the framework of views of God that he has inherited from his Jewish contemporaries?

Jesus' God, we saw, is impartial in causing the sun to shine and the rain to fall on just and unjust alike (Matt 5:45). The divine impartiality is stressed, and that the creator God who sustains the created world plays such an active role is simply assumed; that would be expected of divine powers at that time. There is no mention of excesses of sun or rain that could lead to drought, famines, and floods; these caused distress and doubt then, but no attempt was made to limit the power or the responsibility of the creator God; indeed, Israel's God could be viewed as sending such disasters as punishment, as in the case of the generation of Noah who perished in the Flood (cf. Gen 6–9). When Jesus then goes on to speak of other, smaller-scale disasters (Luke 13:1–5), however, there is no mention of God's activity or of God causing these; instead it is the brutality of the Roman governor, on the one hand, and, presumably, the defective construction of

And Our God?

a tower, on the other, that have caused these tragedies, again with no consideration of the righteousness or unrighteousness of the victims. This is, though, not so much a matter of divine impartiality; it is rather implied that God just let these things happen. Throughout, at any rate, Jesus assumes that he is talking of a personal God who causes certain things to happen, but does not intervene or display the divine judgment on others, despite what God is then supposed to do in the world to come. Such a position would in fact be more easily intelligible if we were talking of some force or power that is responsible for all that happens in the world, but without regard to the moral character of those affected by what happens.

At any rate, we have seen in the sayings of Jesus testimony to the divine benevolence as God provides for the inanimate creation and *a fortiori* will also do so for human beings (Matt 6:30/Luke 12:28). Jesus' teaching on prayer presupposes the willingness of God to give and stresses that those praying should therefore expect to receive the good gifts for which they ask (Matt 7:7–11/Luke 11:9–13). Yet, as we noted above, this all seems a far cry from the God of judgment whom Jesus also proclaims, a dissonance that must surely lead us to question the one or the other view of God, whether Jesus gave expression to only one of them or, more than a little inconsistently, to both.

This confidence of answered prayers presents other problems, too, for it is plain that many prayers, to all appearances, remain unanswered. As long as Jesus' God and that of his contemporaries and our God is omnipotent, modeled on the absolute rulers of the ancient world, this is indeed problematic. Yet if we abandon this model and instead see prayer as an alignment of ourselves and our wills with a benevolent and beneficent force permeating the world, then unanswered prayer remains a disappointment, but it is a disappointment for this force, too, for it means that its will, its goal, is also frustrated, if this force is indeed benevolent and is the sort of force that can be said to have a will. This would be part of the suffering of God, a suffering that is more easily intelligible if prayer and our relation to God and God's relation to us are seen in this way. (If it is of the nature of this power to be discerning and intelligent, it may also see that some of our wishes are better unfulfilled; in that case unanswered prayers are a cause for relief, not suffering, on its part.) It is true that the traditional view of God, with all its inherent anthropomorphism, makes the practice of prayer easier to understand and perform, yet that is a high price to pay if we seek a view of God that has some hope of corresponding to reality, mysterious though that reality may be.

The benevolence of God, we saw, is implied in the provision of sun and rain for all, even if the excesses of these "gifts" is a problem passed over in silence. Something of the same benevolence appears in the story of the vineyard owner who paid his laborers the same wage, whether they had worked a whole day or just one hour (cf. Matt 20:15, "Am I not allowed to do as I choose with what is mine? Or is your eye evil [are you jealous] because I am good [generous]?"), a benevolence and even-handedness, we noted, that would have startled Jesus' hearers as much as they surprise us. That is a reminder that, however much Jesus' thinking and teaching about God was constrained by the assumptions current among his contemporaries,

And Our God?

he could at certain points break free of these constraints. If we have to choose between views that he shared with his contemporaries and what seem to be innovations, and if these two seem to clash—as is the case with the generous and even-handed God and one who judges strictly by deeds in the world to come and is anything but generous in dealing with the wicked—then there is a strong case for preferring the former, while allowing for the possibility that Jesus may have inconsistently combined two incompatible views of God.

Again, Jesus apparently surprised his contemporaries, and offended some of them, by the company he kept, particularly in the case of those with whom he ate. Sometimes we find him at table with more "respectable" company, as when a Pharisee invites him to his house (Luke 7:36), but repeatedly we find him criticized for eating with tax-collectors and sinners. This is offensive, not just because Jesus does it, but because he is the one who claims to be acting and teaching in God's name, with the implication that the welcome he extends to these people, seemingly with no preconditions such as repentance (Zacchaeus' offer of restitution comes *after* Jesus had accepted the invitation to his house: Luke 19:6–8), is a welcome that his God also extends through him. The openness and welcome that Jesus displays in his conduct is implicit, too, in the ministry and preaching of Paul, for, if Jesus welcomed the "sinners" of his Jewish world in God's name, Paul did that as well in preaching God's good news and the offer of entry into the people of God to those whom he had hitherto been accustomed to view with Jewish eyes as "sinners," the non-Jews (Gal 2:15).

The God of Jesus—Our God?

It is scarcely surprising that Jesus' benevolent and generous view of God has also left its mark on his ethical teaching. His followers are to take their moral cue from the character and actions of Jesus' God, or at least the generous and merciful God whom he proclaims. This is clear in the story Jesus told of a servant whose master let him off an astronomically large debt and who then went and threw one of his fellows into prison because he owed him a far more paltry sum. Because the first servant had not shown mercy as his master had shown to him, the forgiveness of his debt is cancelled and he must pay the penalty, imprisoned till he has repaid the last penny (Matt 18:23–35). That we should forgive others as God forgives us is also stressed in the Lord's Prayer in Matthew's version (6:14–15). The God who will judge in the world to come also, of course, plays a role in Jesus' teaching, as is the case in the story of the unmerciful servant just mentioned, but then as a sanction that we may well judge unworthy of the God whose actions and attitudes in this world Jesus has portrayed in teaching, story, and his own actions. When we concentrate on what Jesus taught his followers to do, rather than on the threats that he is shown as uttering against those who fail to do so, then the picture is rather different. His followers are then to act as Jesus himself acted, not just in continuing his ministry of preaching and healing, but also in the way they behave towards one another and others. For Jesus' teaching about God sending sun and rain on righteous and unrighteous alike follows, as we saw, on the command to love one's enemies and pray for one's persecutors, so that his hearers may be children of their heavenly Father who thus blesses righteous and unrighteous (Matt 5:44–45). The following

And Our God?

injunction to be "perfect" as God is perfect (Matt 5:48) may seem overdone, but points in the same direction: God's character should be ours too. It should be clear, however, the character that is meant is that of the forgiving, merciful God, and not that of the God who sends a debtor to prison until he or she has repaid the last penny.

Were it only a matter of being forgiving and merciful like Jesus' God, then this might seem a rather negative way of putting it, but the fellowship Jesus offered and created, as did Paul after him, points in a far more positive direction. It is, namely, the invitation to enter into and form a community that transcends those prejudices and other barriers that normally separate members of the human race from one another and hinder their life together. It is a community based on love, love for one's neighbor as for oneself (Mark 12:31/Matt 22:39; cf. Luke 10:27). That is a reality that can be realized in our world, although its realization has unfortunately hitherto only been but at best fragmentary, even in the community that acknowledges Jesus as its Lord and claims to follow the path he taught his disciples to tread. Yet in those fragments we can see glimpses of the kingly rule of God that Jesus proclaimed and sought to bring about, again fragmentarily. Now it may be that we do not want to recognize there the leading of any divine power, and instead ascribe these fragments of loving community to a human altruism or even an enlightened self-interest that sees that the cost to oneself is ultimately worth it and is willing to transcend those factors that make for human disunity. Or again it may be suggestive that when Albert Schweitzer—at the close of his *The Quest of the Historical Jesus*, that great and influential review of (mostly nineteenth-century) at-

The God of Jesus—Our God?

tempts to write a life of Jesus—tries to say what the life of this man means for his own day, he comes to speak of the continuing influence of the spirit of Jesus. Yet it may also be appropriate to identify this spirit with that of God, or God as spirit, present in and working through Jesus.

In the vision engendered by this ethic we can see what lasting significance Jesus' message of God's rule can have today, both for the individual and collectively. It should be realized that it remains a thoroughly this-worldly ethic and message. And yet for many the world to come and what happens after the individual's death remains of obsessive and overwhelming importance. Despite Paul's seeming endorsement of this view and concern, that may be mistaken as was noted earlier, and Jesus' followers are right to concentrate their attention on this world and its demands, its possibilities, and its needs. Yet the realities of this world should not be viewed through rose-tinted glasses, and the extent to which they fall woefully short of the righteousness and peace for which Jesus strove and ultimately died confronts his followers with a constant challenge to work for the realization of that vision.

That is very much a concern and an agenda for this world. What of the world to come if there is one? Now the twenty-third Psalm, for instance, is one that for many embodies the very essence of Israel's piety, quite apart from the moving beauty of its imagery, and yet one cannot help asking whether it is not beset by an excessive complacency and a confidence that bears little relation to the experience of life of very many:

> The Lord is my shepherd, I shall not want. . . .
>   he restores my soul.
> He leads me in right paths for his name's sake.

And Our God?

> Even though I walk through the darkest valley,
> I fear no evil, for you are with me; your rod
> and staff—they comfort me. . . .
> Surely goodness and mercy shall follow me all
> the days of my life, and I shall dwell in the
> house of the Lord my whole life long.
> (Ps 23:1, 3–4, 6, New Revised Standard Version)

This psalm seems to betray an excessive optimism about life in this world at least. For how many of those who trust in this God did and do in fact suffer want? How many find their souls or spirits seemingly unbearably crushed? How many have found themselves to have strayed from "the right paths"? How many can actually say that goodness and mercy have followed them *all* the days of their lives? Here the psalmist seems to have been blessed with an experience of life that is granted to few. The fourth verse, which perhaps accounts for the popularity of this psalm at funerals (for some versions read here "the valley of the shadow of death"), may not do justice to the dread with which some in fact approach their death. And yet, on the other hand, as I argued in a study of the resurrection narratives of the New Testament, what many, myself included, at least in cultural circles no longer dominated by fears of judgment beyond the grave, approach with more foreboding is the path leading to a death that may actually be seen as a liberation. Now, if faith in God turns out to be, after all, an illusion, we have nothing to fear beyond the grave, where we shall at last find rest. If, on the other hand, there is a God, a mysterious Other, however inscrutable the divine nature may be, then let that God be the God of Jesus, at least that God whom Jesus proclaimed as merciful and benevolent, sending blessing on good and evil alike, enduring with the good and evil whatever suffering the world inflicts upon them, but not the God the view of whose nature Jesus took over from the beliefs of his contemporaries, a God who inflicts suffering and punishment in a world to come. If God is indeed merciful and benevolent, then whatever form of contact with that Other may be possible beyond the grave, there is indeed no cause for fear, and the presence of that God, however we experience it, *will* be a comfort.

For Further Reading

I have dealt in some earlier works and in more detail with a number of the themes and questions touched on here, in particular:

Beyond Resurrection. London: SCM, 1999.

Jesus and the Historians. WUNT 269. Tübingen: Mohr Siebeck, 2010.

The Death of Jesus: Some Reflections on Jesus-Traditions and Paul. WUNT 299. Tübingen: Mohr Siebeck, 2013.

www.ingramcontent.com/pod-product-compliance
Lightning Source LLC
Chambersburg PA
CBHW022119090426
42743CB00008B/921